one crossed out

one ~~crossed~~ out

FANNY HOWE

GRAYWOLF PRESS

Publication of this volume is made
possible in part by a grant provided
by the Minnesota State Arts Board
through an appropriation by the
Minnesota State Legislature, and by
a grant from the National Endow-
ment for the Arts. Significant addi-
tional support has been provided by
the Andrew W. Mellon Foundation,
the Lila Wallace-Reader's Digest
Fund, the McKnight Foundation,
and other generous contributions
from foundations, corporations, and
individuals. To these organizations
and individuals who make our work
possible, we offer heartfelt thanks.

Published by Graywolf Press
2402 University Avenue, Suite 203
Saint Paul, Minnesota 55114
All rights reserved.

www.graywolfpress.org

Published in the
United States of America

ISBN 1-55597-259-4

2 4 6 8 9 7 5 3 1
First Graywolf Printing, 1997

Library of Congress Catalog Card
Number: 97-70217

Cover design: Jeanne Lee
Cover art: Italo Scanga

"There Are No 'Others'"—
Variation on the lyrics from
"What Kind of Fool Am I?"
by Leslie Bricusse and Anthony
Newley, © 1961 Essex Music Ltd.

Grateful acknowledgment is made to the
editors of the following publications in
which the poems below first appeared:

AGNI:
  "Finish"
Grand Street:
  "Start"
  "Basic Science"
  "The Apophatic Path"
Hambone:
  "Victory"
O'blek:
  "Perfection and Derangement"
Out West:
  "Parallel"
  "Bathroom"
  "Starlet"
Parentheses:
  "[sic]"
Ploughshares:
  "The Low Road"
  "Everything's a Fake"
  "The Bourgeoisie Despises Poverty . . ."
  "You Can't Warm Your Hands . . ."
  "My Song, My Only Song Goes:"
Raddle Moon:
  "One Crossed Out"
TriQuarterly:
  "Plutocracy"

Many thanks to the California Arts Council
and the National Endowment for the Arts.

for Linda—
(then, now and on)—
no words

one crossed out

Start

When Adam the Billionth
called the sky's name
he was like someone who believed
his voice made him a magician.

Psychoanalysis had no cure—
and neither did America—for his error.
Nothing! he shouted
and the print this word left in the air

was as gray as moonstuff
and the world was dimmer for it.
We shall all fall into Tophet
like ice off of fruit

before anyone answers to that name.

Basic Science

One cadaver said to the other
cadaver, "You're my cadaver."

The conversation ended there
but not its effects.

Their souls had evaporated.

It was up to love to raise them
from their litters and let them

arrive as the living poor
at the surface of earth. It did.

At first the maculate pair
poked and picked through refuse.

Denials were their daily breads.
Then they were sold to those

who found their fertility a bonus.
Owned then by the living with names

and fortunes, with lovers who say,
"Lover, I'm your lover,"

cadavers were still the majority.
They kept creation going and love

as well—like hands on a cold
or sunburned back—a weight

with properties that animate.

Finish

A fin de siècle echoing fuck:

up through hotel walls, two-bed poverty.
From the trolley at T.J.

to the old port and green stairway
past a small café, I was my own army.

Outside the conference hall
(where ideals were my orders)

there was rain and if I was to get home ever
I had to come inside to confirm my reservation.

Over the asphalt gray drops blew
and when the ink had dried under fluorescent lights

I returned—by rail—
to the Free World, or whatever it's called.

The Advance of the Father

From raindrenched Homeland into a well: the upturned animal
was mine by law and outside the tunnel, him again!
Everywhere I turned the children ran between. "Loose dogs!"
he roared. I remember one sequence: a gulf in his thinking
meant swim as fast as you can. But it was winter and the water
was closed. The mouths of the children were sealed with ice.
After all, we were swimming in emotion, not water.

"Shut up! you Father!" I shouted over my shoulder. Racing,
but not spent, my mind went, "It isn't good that the human being
is all I have to go by. . . . It isn't good that I know who I love
but not who I trust. . . . . It isn't good that I can run to a priest
but not to a plane. . . . I lost my way exactly like this."

Inverted tunnel of the self.
Throat or genital search for the self.
Light that goes on in the self when the eyes are shut.
Uniformity impossible in the psyche's pre-self
like a day never spent, or how the unseen can make itself felt.

It was as if a boy was calling from the end of a long island.
Docks were vertical and warlike.
I would be on one side of my bed like a mother who can tell
she's a comfort because she's called Mother.
Still, we both would be able to see the edge of the problem.

It's true that the person is also a thing.
When you are running you know the texture. I was clawing
at the palm of one hand and brushing up my blues with the other.
A man who wore his boxers at night remarked that my daughter
was tired. He had nothing to do with anything.

Ahead was the one with magnified eyes and historical data to last.
Know-how and the hysteria to accomplish his whole life.
It was horrible what we would do for peace.
We told him the story of the suffering he made us feel
with the ingratiating stoop of those who came second in the world.

Victory

There is no Rescue Mission where it isn't freezing
from the need that created it. The lost children

distill to pure chemical. Where Good is called No-Tone
it's the one who cries out who doesn't get a coat.

The children fuse colors because they don't want to
separate. Daughters shot off of hydrants who cut

each other in the neck and gut, don't care
which one of them will end up later in surgery.

And drugged sons pretending to be costumes,
well, they're not welcome to comprehension either.

Why does a wild child confuse a moon
with a hole in his skin?

One was born soaked in gin.
His first sip was from a bottle of denial.

What can "leave me alone" mean after that?
The system is settled, dimensions fixed.

Another one's hand feels like a starfish.
Makes me hysterical like the word *perestroika*.

But they all dig the way the pepper is rosy in the vodka.
It's verbocity that creates jokers.

Brick and grit are the candy and frosting
where volunteers and teachers write cards that go:

"Donate books that say NOT and NO and poets
who say Um instead of Oh."

How do the children convert their troubles
into hip-hop? Dunno—but it's wonderful.

My Broken Heart

On the 85th night of 19— there were 280 days left in the year.
The cure began. Just as Pascal carried the date of his revelation
in his breast pocket, I began to carry a dated hanky next to my heart.
Healing is a job that requires a mop.

This arm I am leaning on is perfectly suited to mine.
(I always wanted to say that.) Now cold winds have come
and the doctor has determined that my hope was full of holes.
"But holes in the universe are made of matter."

On the 305th night of 19— there were 60 days left in the year.
The cure began. Beauty of style depends on similarity.
Snow for instance is a perfect show, because the sky
opens like a flower shaking out its secrets.

This time of year reminds me of the dot that completes my name.
The dot over the letter that pertains to the first person
singular is a symbol for me of my head.
I always put on my dot when I'm already out of the word.

At last I only have hope for heaven.
Like a person who has "come to" after fainting,
I now know the meaning of the question:
"Where in the world?"

Women should sit down like me—
wherever they are standing now—and refuse to move.
I always wanted to say that.
Whoa! Is someone here, or is this, like, a hat tossed in the air?

Am I really better at being crushed than I was before?

Plutocracy

If you have no expectations, you can't be disappointed.
A SURVIVOR OF HURRICANE ANDREW

1

After the storm the word WATER kept rising
and circling the color oil.
The snow of the ocean blued and whirled.
There was water in all the machinery.
Waves knocked a water tower into a boat thrown off-course
by the hurricane. A ruined deck and dock, trees
uprooted from the heaving ground.

2

Gloved and cycling, the worker leaves the house.
His forehead is gleaming like David's.
The ground can hear his motions, the grass divides.
Pink hibiscus in the mist: for many like him all this
has been hellish. Compressed by the cosmos, not embraced,
he knows the dread that can't say yes.

3

It's as if money's eyes are located inside a pyramid.
Unfit for the rest of human habitation. Not like a cone,
generously spilling, he decides,
passing a blind couple walking, sighted child between.
Hard-luck stories are never boring.

4

After a storm there's a powerless period, when the word
POWER keeps repeating, and when will the clock go on
in the kitchen and the trees finish falling in the mind?

He recalls his mother
whose days have the resonance of drums
played on the shins of a lazy teen. Her nouns
are thoughtless as shoes to be worn till the soles
of the feet show. To begin again where?
Near the pink dollop at the back of the tongue.

5

The playing field is disheveled.
his anger's target is on his way to a party
near the drive-by harbor slow-boated by boys
in motorized canoes. His power is out.
Only cars fathom the between, obsolete as soon as seen.
Nothing tech can stay: rust of entropy edges even
a bloated bike tire laid out on a stump.

6

The worker's mother was always seeking the problem
behind the fix
and wanting him to solve it. With thread on her lip
she, at home after work, nagged him.
Meanwhile an orderly twilight inks the twinkles
and the mathematics of stillness

is holiest when everyone is changing for bed, or in it.
If a star is in her eye, she knows the star
is finding itself, there, in her eye. Enlightenment
is a level without measurement.

7

The worker played king on a bike through seven gates
where trees lead to capitalist parties, cocktails

and the kitsch of four cultures. The maid
washed the dishes and spat in the chocolate.
Fill in the blank where that man stood
not a day earlier as Everylove to this woman
at the end of her bed. Her maintenance since then:
the wind, emptying—an emotion to lean on.
Often in her melon yellow uniform
melancholy wouldn't quit her till she hit the kitchen
and the dishes waiting to pay her.

8

Summer of the linoleum tulips.
Storm entropied into drips. She will, for days
after the gale winds blow over, bear fruit
and bag her own vegetables. Friendship
she offered others into the moon-hours, drink from
supernatural grapes and potatoes.
Rubber slicked on asphalt under the branches,
saws attacked the remnants of trees. Her psyche cracked
where a mirror made the candle brighter.

9

She is making a cake in the post-storm kitchen.
Outside champagne rains air in a bottle.
Desire simulates fire as sure as she has heard a voice
in her ear call her. The head at her feet—
the eyes in her palm—the supplicant dishes look up—

indications of Saint Monica wanting to appear
in her consciousness. Ordinary time's daily prayer
for the conversion of workers to angels.
But only pure prayer makes the air into an ear.

10

After the storm, the long-limbed oak trees twist. Corkish.
They drank in kitchen wicker, and watched.
Are those half-people or chairs at a bar? He held her
ankles with his feet.
People are begotten from eternity, only to be returned.
And the animals of Paradise?
Let fortune smile on them! Or: send someone to burn
these monsters up. A person worthy of a sparrow's ashes.
Together one night they hosed down his anger, and learned
that a wound is only the edge of self-awareness.

11

At the capitalist party, the eros of a dress suggesting tips
reinforces the connection between pyramids and money. Corks
are unplugged from the green, which is then drunk with the
savage concentration of bees wanting honey from a color.
Gossip evolves like a sour ball
growing smaller in a mouth.

12

Apparatus, don't be embarrassed by my life
as a dishwasher. In an undeveloped tract, I too thought
about meaning and the body as a bit of technology.
This put my little coffin aloft in a whirl of stars
with the origin of numbers.

What if we destroy the earth?
What if I am never again touched?
What if the weak are overcome?

What if winning is a sign of God's love?
What if women made men so mean?

13

When you eat alone you don't exist
for anyone but the dish.
Like the spaniel (the dog of invincible obsession)
you might stare fixedly into a water glass for hours.

14

Sometimes eros appears in sleeping ears as the prayers
of the flesh, empty of consciousness.
And then the candle's wax peels off its hot body
like foreskin. And you find yourself
entering the long loneliness.

15

He held his bike between his thighs to contemplate
the damage. The power of water. "If I were given access
to several facts, I might finally mobilize
a people's army to rise against the problematics.
But anonymity is the true goal of my democracy."

16

She could have backed up into the target of the worker's anger
and done violence. Assassinate. One giant step
would accomplish it.
That arm even extended over her shoulder,
not interested in contact, colder than a barber
at Treblinka. He was the right temperature
for those who kill by proxy. But she believed
in the immortal soul and hesitated.

What if the rosary is a heresy?
What if the world is divine?

What if hell is a permanent state of mind?
What if the saints live in outer space?
What if a Jesus does too?

17

After the storm, the sun is drying seaweed,
winds dying over Toronto,
cloud formations gold as print.
On the West Coast
the sand has the hue of a burned lion.
Whispering sandmen say the hurricane is gone—
shelters for periwinkle and people—can be closed again.
And into the ears of babies, prayers
take a circular turn.

18

Scissors cut up the tree's meat.
Chickenish interior ripped by hurricane winds.
Everywhere people struggle
to be individuated in company. They pay for everything.
Sere leaves of August are used as window decorations.
Plates drip with oil like recreational vehicles
in the harbor. The temptation to poison
the plutocrats is a goal for the underling
to play bone with.

19

Now an asteroid the size of an island is heading towards
earth. When is Daddy coming home?
The anxious daughter on the doorstep
tips to see the path bend. She might as well wonder,
Who loves me better than the dog?
Do women's thoughts really scatter?

20

From the porch, across the grass stacked with firewood,
the worker waves with the confidence of every owner
or assassin in a rush. He'll note aluminum siding
on the way to the crime and remember:
>No windows in the ark.
>Keep out the view of water.
>It would drive them mad to see the power of water.

21

After the storm, for her on the cliff, smoking
above Makonikey Cove,
the curl of a shell studded with barnacles, is the same
size as the mainland.
Like a quartz clock ticking through a storm,
or a tennis game in rain,
her heart patters on under the sweat of her thinking.

What if I am, as he said, ordinary?
What if the universe knows more than humans do?
What if knowledge is only knowledge of God?
What if there is no escape from our ignorance?
What if there is no escape from existence?

22

A body's interior is a serpent studded with corruption.
From the will of each person—to secret egos—
she sees a net, dot-to-dot, interconnected, with persons
bent over it, laborious, intent, the whole world
working together on one collective project.

When your mouth remembers a bit of bread
left on a plate and leads you back to finish it,

you are having the experience—
close to the surface—by which you usually live.

23

There is no isthmus to Chappaquiddick
but a bridge sitting close to the water in broken pieces
of night. Blue and silver lights
dip into the surface.

24

I bet it's been computed
down to the footsteps and the sacrifice of a dog.
I bet it's loaded already: the pace of each car,
ocean voyages, office work, oil slicking birds
like Tarbaby's image. What's the definition
of capitalism? Sink or swim.
What's the definition of Apocalypse? Time.

25

Let's start an anarchist party. The worker-assassin folds up
his knees with milk and cookie on one,
waiting for something like Krishna's news
to come over the air. Will salvation come through a box,
a mouth, or through shoes? He can't delight
in the stuffed feeling of being a person
except when he's empty, then greed is good.

26

Meanwhile the servant woman, her hands in suds,
remembers her own case: mud across a penitentiary yard:
omens, like lawyers coming, in the shape of electric light
on puddles. Artificial light should never burn near water.

Daughters in jail are often mothers and sisters sit for each
other. Only labor cares about her body in the world.

If I had a form that fit my nature
I didn't know it.
Thread on my tongue—grow thin—when I get home—

for the needle in my fingers.
Don't make me struggle.

What if I am never found by God?
What if I am disfigured by my acts?
What if I bear bad fruit?
What if I have to live this way for the rest of my life?
What if I never change?

27

If it was something corresponding to the ark;
and if it was Jung's dream of a holocaust on a train;
and if it was a democracy of poetry leveled into prose;
and if it was that night again:
and if the man was laughing on the wall;
and if the woman falling under the car away from her son;
if it was a gray wind called—;
if we were crossed by:
or if it was the return of the;
and if the cows cost;
and if it was east to;
and a hurricane blew over their;
then it wasn't; the fault; of anything.

28

He said of his life so far: "It was me and it was about me.
My time was a mystery, but it was mine.
I wish I remembered more."

29

The assassin crossed the unfinished palace
with no voice, no vote, his whole body logged. He is willing
his things to the people, in his mind.
The wind and the plunk of old rain, like puncturing ballots
with pins behind curtains, are beating him on.

He was a kind of innocent wearing the vestments of sin.
My fathers were women, he was often saying.

30

He knew to sit with his dish on one knee
watching TV while a woman was waiting
to wash up after him.
Let's not call it a party, but an army, he told her.

31

It's the end of a year of slaughter.
Jesus of the Sacred Chrism
and Black Jesus of the Poison, Jesus of the Secret Life,
Jesus of the Cursing Lips, Jesus of the Broken Hands,
and Jesus of all the Millions of Children
drinking chemical water . . .
in a year heaven is supposed to move closer,
or the minds of humans are going to grow higher . . .
as the water rises, so does the boat.

32

Levels will be unaccountable in the windowless ark.
What looks like an olive will be filled with prickles.
Nativity starts with a boat and a baby forever,
with rushes licking a woman's waterbank. What is the light
around such bondage? Slaves and babies,
zero eyes, the surprise of the good.

33

After the storm, a fragile boat, welded to a wall
of water, floats backwards over the gray water, with rain
attached like threads to a tapestry.
The statue of Lenin has fallen on its side
becoming a garden ornament after a storm.
And if this is a ballad, its refrain is secret.

34

Misery maintenance, cold pipe of the radiated
rain. Down to stone, gravel, and ladder,
out the kitchen window, she spoke of pastel water.
But what is it really? The orange is over the snack bar.
And tonight the sleepless hers will give away their slick
desires to illness, cramp, perverse renunciations
of the heart to others. It's a Via Negativa: no way EVER
to have both an honorable and youthlike power.

35

What if, she said to the man, *I never meet a worthy man?*
And what if I really do die in the end?

The Gerard Manley Hopkins in her thinking
made him listen. He was called outside to fix
a broken line, to get the lights going again.

36

I want the world to be good, is the only thing.

37

You have to bend the bitterness with markings
and tragic erotics, in order to get yourself straight again.
After the storm the earth is running down,
it's turned the entropy up. He sees
from the top of a pole that givers and payers are one
person. Takers and debtors are too.
Sins of criminals and assassins hold no candle
to the issue of justice, which is also too big to see.

38

The technology of his tool makes a worker unable to murder
with it. Could a carpenter wound with a nail?
Is it supernatural if you can't put a name to a shadow?
Her questions kill his will to kill.
Telegraph, telegram, telephone—
three cruciforms declaring ALONE.
The man was hanging like an obsolete puppet, or
like the second to win. The wind pulls the strings.
And the lights go on.

39

Beside the mountain ocean, speed of snow
is the foam-bubbling light, green.
The priceless wet-side
is like a benign wall through a tunnel
of appetites made lacy, and abstract.

THE END:

When she sees his eyes later—red and swollen
and faraway, she remembers the symmetry of the stars
at night, and whispers freely,
I don't know what to do with the poetry.
I don't know what to do with my body.
He tells her she has done it already.

Perfection and Derangement

Dirt road, down a slope. In spring the trees are spackled with white blossoms, some flecks of pink. The branches look like long bones; the white has returned to them in the form of snow. Pinker berries dot the thinnest branches and thorns, and a spray of same lies across the rotted porch. If you look through the boarded-up windows you will see a contraption for restraining someone too sad to move.

Where can I rest? Satellites circle this snow-covered flatland. Orchards are bare by the reservoir, the green benches bent from cold. Under the ice I can see a leaf, a can, a tire, a fish, something from outer space. Then the water hardens like gelatin, swollen into lumps where old leaves are inlaid. An interior, destroyed by mismanagement.

Suffering is how the world informs the human mind that it is there. Suffering proves to the mind that it is exposed to alien substance, like it or not. If you can't act even while you suffer, you can only suffer and sink. Nonetheless a person has a right to protest and complain and to yearn bitterly for release.

May for one rejects any absolute dualism. She has it that past, present, and future exist simultaneously. All time is the ONE's creation. Then police from Rhode Island call and want to know her status. They say they found her walking along the highway in shirtsleeves with no money, on her way to New York. They have brought her to the Cranston Medical Center and she can be picked up there.

Women are like roaches, they survive so much. They seem to grow tougher with each succeeding generation. I think the evolution of material things came before the entrance of women onto this earth, but they followed almost immediately. The first one was last seen through a hole in the clouds, going down through the top. A kind of intergalactic-storm reviewer, she jumped directly for the heart and support.

Where are you that you don't invite me in, turning your hand out and over? Do you know which room I inhabit, the bed among beds and under stone joinings? That none of these belong to me?

"To confabulate is to conceal your mental retardation. To confabulate is to be a fool filling in the gaps in your memory with detailed accounts of false events."

What do you dream about in the facility? Will you ever wake up to the facts and this way give up HOPE?

Your hands, like ten virtues, can only do so much. I have noticed, since coming here, that each person in this world is chasing his or her self at all times. Some people just move slower getting from the past person to the present or first one. Those who wail they want to go home are referring to a community where justice prevails and they get their mail. Though they are certainly sociopathic, they're not in prison, are they? They were never violent, but more likely terrified.

Our primordial metaphysical and religious experience begins in terror. This produces a modesty whose secret is only revealed through certain sacraments and only to those participating in them. This transaction is called THE DISCIPLINE OF THE SECRET.

I had just figured out how to live correctly when I realized it was too late, I had taken too long figuring it out.

Before onrushing time I experience total helplessness. Like the words, "You shall see my back but my face shall not be seen," the beauty of a human face belongs to its turning away.

Likewise for every one fact there's a second one to counter it. If therefore I knew all the facts, I would be paralyzed—on wheels again at last.

The hidden countenance is one countenance worth contemplating. There a felicitous light swells into substance, which sees as you see and breathes as you breathe; it even kisses where you kiss. Whisper your prayers if you want to call it out of the dark.

You asked me what I know about G–d and coincidence. I walk through you to tell you, the place where you stood like an opening in the form of an offering.

The soul originates in fire, cooperative and quick. It deteriorates into a self by becoming stiff and slow moving. Now a place becomes a space suitable only for walking and the self often trails behind the body like a shadow. Better to feel your soul is rushing ahead of you than that your self is limping behind.

Colors return and scandalize the objects that were happily hidden. My position has changed. I've moved back to make room for the whole view, but still it's from that corner I see the space that held you.

I have failed to view my actions as having any importance, have spread myself thinly across the tops of things. I have resisted change, a new way of doing or thinking about the world. I have not lived up to the hopes anyone had for me. It makes me sick.

It's true that May had escaped in the morning and was returned by guards in the afternoon, saying *Because I had nowhere to go.* Now she is just sitting down in a dazed state. Inappropriate laughter as usual. She was very upset about the commitment proceedings. Her sister really hates her.

Why all the emphasis on lobbies? Paul asked me. I told him that they can be shortcuts to streets. I didn't want him to know that every lobby is private, so the homeless have one less place to congregate. The Department of Mental Health should have a terraced waterfall cascading down the stairs to show visitors how it feels being scared.

Come here and fill the space waiting.
May I lick your lips?
Any opinion on the defense budget?
Come here, never. You can rest there in the open door.
Three songs—refrigerator, birds, and a trolley start at 5 A.M.

Bend to get the hint: there have been advances in cruelty since Oliver Twist.

Poor Paul called the sky Tubby. Snow, Tubby, he would say.

Anyone ordering restraints in this place has got to be familiar with the way it feels on the other side. I carry a little glass ball on a thread as my refuge and my joy. I do the lights, or did, every year on the facility green. I put the spotlight on dogs. It was often foggy in December. And I bet Christmas Eve wouldn't have eaten that apple if it had been that foggy. She wouldn't have been able to see it in the first place.

What will you give me to leave you since I haven't begun to die yet? I'm sorry. My mother would always say, "You get more excited by Christmas than any child I know." That showed how much she loved me before she left me in Valley Forget. We had a duplex with all the amenities, including hardwood floors, central air-conditioning, fireplace, private roof deck, a Euro-style kitchen, and a ranch-style living room. It was amazing. Ma kept a table set and waiting all day every day. When I had time I'd grab a hot dog and cola and sit right down in front of a display of china and silver. No matter if I wolfed down my lunch. I appreciated every bite in that environment.

Tonight the ward is quiet. People have a zombie attitude and seem only inwardly hostile. Sam oiled his hair with toothpaste before bed. I had seven vacancies and fourteen beds. Some of these people are ready for another redeemer, I tell you. Every event is packed with hidden meaning.

I said we won't accept a lenient sentence since evil is built into our system. Sustained, said Your Honor. I can't help worrying, though, we're so broke. No awnings, no boat hulls or sails, no automobile panels, no water skis, no beverage bottle carriers, no covers for cushions or appliance handles, to name just a few.

No family, no friends.
In the shelter hot meals are liable to clang. Eyes are like primitive telescopes facing the sea. I've been in that trick fortress too long. Someone is always fucking following me. There's no safety.

May is now acting very strangely, staring at the ceiling rigidly, tongue-in-cheek. She saw two red nails in a door that gave her a sign of Christ. Later when she was staring at the ceiling she said the holes in it looked as though they were breathing!

Now the snow is going up and down, now it is waving to the side. The branches seem to lift into zebra-snakes asking for food from the cloaked fir trees. The sky is solid white. A full moon will be rising, pink, and close to the horizon soon, and will polish the night shapes.

What was lost, comes back—like May—but how do we know we are not already somebody's tomorrow? Am I here and waiting, the table set and the toast warm for someone alive in a yesterday?

I was kicked out of Ma's apartment a month after she left, so I don't know if she came home again. She left me a note beginning, *Dear Reality*, and signed, *Love, Me*. The man who kicked me out of the apartment was so greedy I bet he would appraise the value of a walnut shell if an ant wanted to live there.

Is G–d a place that it should move with me in my car? Or is this ability to move a sign that it's not a place at all? The ONE experiences itself through its creation, even though it existed before and beyond that creation, I'm told. The ONE is lonely and loves voices that call to it, even when it can do nothing to help but only sympathize.

Likewise the soul informs the body of its presence but doesn't really have an effect on acts.

Stop feeling sorry for May when she's put in seclusion. At 7 A.M. she assaulted poor Sam in his wheelchair, hitting him with her fist several times on the back of the head. When the nurse came with meds to her room, she threw them back at her and became assaultive again. Was given 100 mg of Thorazine and was quiet for the rest of the night. If you feel sorry for her it's like saying that G–d has abandoned her. Imagine how that makes her feel. Just try to help her out instead.

It's all very well for you to say you don't know G–d, but what would you say if you learned that G–d doesn't know YOU?

May said, I lost my self-control. It just got away from me. Later it came out as a splash of color here, twelve smears of gray there, oak trees shot in morbid details, the hum of a cello, words overheard, and a pirouette. I think that each one now is the signature of a lost person looking for a home—not a shelter—a home like the one that was promised to us somewhere along the line.

[sic]

"If your shadow can't live at its full length, then you suffer.
Hell has no shadows and neither does the hell-maker.
When I first woke up in this world there were no shadows
that I could see, but a pair of hands, eyes, and the outside
of her skin."

"I felt like a face in a towel, confused, soiled.
Mayflowers in the Cape woods were pink and shivering,
the size of snowdrops, the day the blood let fall.
They moved like my brain when it thinks of the Holy One
and goes, no, no, NO."

"Female offenders have a tendency to study their hands
for weeks on end. Strawlike heads are bent, gales of hay
laughing and rolling down the meadows outside in the wind."

"Pink is hidden, yellow is prison. One day—BLAM
to all my hopes. I was as low as a coward and the stones
could have my bones."

"If a warden looks at you and makes you feel guilty
by that look, you are allergic to authority."

Sucking the cover of a bone
the notch formed a well.

Bottle of spittle
warmed between your thighs.

I ran on wine
all hour driven into forward

like a dream held up careening
to the terminus of dread.

I have to leave my spirit here
smoke out like a morning guest.

But first step up this quest
of thirst. To the set facts, drink.

"In those days my voice pretended to be me, the way each
one of my thoughts begins in my mind but ends up out
there, where it never meets others like it. When I
grabbed hold of things, they rejected me. There was at first
a surfeit of angles. By now I know each one by heart."

"Why do we have pubic hair anyway? To teach us modesty.
There really is no normal pattern for bowel movements
in life or in jail. If diarrhea persists for more than forty-eight
hours, though, they will send you to a clinic
where you'll receive the tender touches of a nurse.
The officers decide if you are worthy or not—that is, sick
enough—to receive this favor."

"For better or worse I know every room, every exit,
every loose stone in this prison.
It depends on what you want but a true expert knows
the exceptions better than the rules. Find an enlightened
criminal and I will show you a potential revolutionary.
Courage is often placed in the wrong heart and the wrong
     part of town."

"I called my boyfriend in Queens and a woman answered
the phone saying, *It's lucky I'm not the jealous type.*
I asked for a home-confinement order, but I had concurrent
terms and a record of *incendiary ideals* that kept me in my place.
Too bad. I would have killed her."

My breasts depressed me when the suck
wore off. The no-self ate me up.

Dogs ran at my heels and a pram
braked on sand.

I never get what I want. I wined
and dined instead. When I have to struggle

to win some money or love
it just means trouble.

I have babied the mother enough, Mum.

"*Never try to stop a rolling car*, I told a retarded friend,
or you'll get your hands squashed. Believe it or not,
he did it anyway."

"They said, you CHOSE to get pregnant twice. You CHOSE
to get bored in the factory. You CHOSE to drop out of school.
It's no one's fault you ended up here, so why complain?
And I wasn't even complaining when they said these things."

"Serve your time and get rid of your crime, they tell me now.
I say, *Solid God, let them know that they are serving time
too, only they don't know why.*"

*She lies in her cell and pretends she's in a courtyard
made of white, green, and black marble and there's a
circular skylight and fountain there, ribbed vaulting,
glass at night with reflected light back into the space
below where he stands, hand-in-hand with her, and her
face is turned up under the shadows of a baseball cap,
she's trashed, and they're seeking fusion, which will
burst the edges of their skin.*

First it's sweet to suck
and then it's sin.

On the whale-road heading south
—all the whitecaps stiff—

I longed for a lick of the drip
you left on the bottle

unable to see what was in it
or your eyes

while the redcap fizzed the stuff.

"Why did I confess my crime to those white-collar
criminals, the winners? They only thought I was a fool
when I did and laughing like trolley tracks threw me in
jail. Then they tortured me because of my stupidity.
They never give a shit about the crime unless the victim
is one of THEM. If it's one of mine, they could care less.
They torture me to feel the pain. It's much like sex,
much. Touch as in *ouch*."

"When we get through the door and make the arrest
one cop told me, *we get a rush that must be something
like the one you guys get off of committing the crime."*

"After studying law I became aware that three
qualities were imperative for trustworthiness,
especially in a white person: lack of self-interest,
low ideals, and good manners."

"I know them. They are the winners out there, ambitious
to a point where only their flesh and blood matters.
Nothing is lower than a white-collar criminal but that is
what they are. They came into my apartment armed with warrants.
Red light, two cars, deep blue flashes. It was hell.
Most guards like angels keep such a low profile, you walk
through them. They turn away from your weaker moments
and prefer not to see what is happening. This was NOT
one of those occasions. I felt that heaven was very close
to earth and there was no space between here and the afterlife.
All judgment was attached to action.
There was NO WAY OUT of anywhere."

"My brother left home in the spirit of an ambassador
to the moon. Later we did unearth one clue: he died.
Children on tiptoes feel the way I do most of each day,
mingling among
the repeat violators, unrehabilitated, smoking and sour.
If I couldn't look through the window of the television,
I would break all my fingers on the stones."

"Where I am is one thing, but where I am NOT is bigger.
The real difficulty is seeing what you are not doing.
You understand nothing of your actual location but move
around with a sense of uneasiness, because only motion
itself can alleviate this anxiety that persists, no matter
what names you choose to give it. The moral religious
names are effective at times; but the psychological, never."

"My daddy made me shovel pig manure so I wouldn't think
in those grand terms. A person shouldn't linger but hunger
after truth, which is food and booze, he liked to tell me.
All you can face in this world is what's got pleasure built in.
It's a discipline."

"My cellmate was shot twice, once in the left eye, once
in the cheek. She spat the bullet out and gave her sister
(shot too) mouth-to-mouth, which failed."

You see I move
lips down, sucking up, the green bottle
shakes cockily.

I see your past
steps, witness from one chair

and note an electric
you in a sequence. You drift,

I count the pace of our rift.
The sucker's position

has made me into the Huck of women.

"I drove this guy through a storm of paintwater.
We couldn't put one and one together but we knew our hearts
like the blues. Those were the nights. Out of prison
my open hand was all his on the rough arm of urban. Graph
marks on his big palm showed nothing was going to end for us
soon on the way to the world's third try. He said, 'Where
a broken line meets heartbeats along the mount to solitude,
lift up your fist for freedom in the five-fingered light.'
He really did. He had a split between his two front teeth
and a Cupid's bow in his upper lip as deep as the swelling
below it. Now I pin his image in my cage and it seems to sing
like a bluebird on a sungold poster. When needs are made known,
they become hideous unless they are served. Worse than hideous,
they are TOLERABLE BURDENS."

Widowed and unwed mother
of the prisoner and liberator,
the homeless, dying, condemned,
executed, refugee and seeker of sanctuary—
pray for us
pray for me—Mary, Maria, Blessed Madre!

"Just give me a chance to act, once, with absolutely reckless
certainty—for somebody else! The victim is at least given
the chance to act with dignity for one last minute, but the animal
has to restore her soul over a lifetime of conversions."

"Mama, do push-ups and thank you for the sardines and crackers
—and cigarettes. But I won't be a good girl ever. You know that.
When poverty comes in at the door, please leap out the window.
I miss you but I've got to say I never knew where the value
of my life really lay until it was too late, away, small as the stars
within my cosmic gaze." Signed Me.

Parallel

Never out of, or into time so deep, as to justify staying this close
    to childhood,
she nonetheless does. A hot-water bottle on her belly,
a book on her head, she is finally convinced that the will to power
belongs to the healthy and the strong.

From her fever she sees little women gather their scarves close
out on the streets. Trucks weigh in when the signs are up on
    the freeway.
She's in a sweat of bewilderment.

The self-multiplication that comes with walking gives her
    the impression
that time flows down in bands.
So don't tell me I have no self. In each one, I stand
complete, sufficient to the prison. I think the soul (self?) is a globe
of placenta-like stuff whose unifying but individuated substance
has its own five senses.

"Excuse me. But could you tell me the way to the day before I was sick
and born??"

She seeks her childhood in the hotel radio. The Zenith lightning rod
once accompanied her on her days home from school. In sixth grade
she was zero times late and twelve times absent. Her feverish anxiety
continues to make her restless. America is so uncomforting,
a person has to keep moving from city to city in search of a numb
    position.

I have a deep experience of nature even though imagination (science)
tells me nothing is there. I am never lonelier than when I am sick.
A person's formula is 70% water and the rest is light.
My soul yearns for an external space it knows.

Home was once a bed like this, a book like this, a red rubber bottle
like this, this view of snow on the wrinkled trunk of an elephant.
Hiss and bang of heat in the voices. So being near pain puts her
    near home,
away from exile's worser hells: infection, institution.

It's like she doesn't look out the window.
She looks at what's on the window.

Bathroom

On certain days a sweat folds in over her, covering her as weather covers a little city. Ghosts of dogs still bark. A man stumbles, dodging a flake. Pink rubbish rises to meet him and burns his cheek. Snow she says is ash from the sun's fire. On the apophatic path being is having. It's where I move even though I can't.

Today she feels she is permanently everywhere she has been and must return to inhabit the same spaces before it's too late. But there is something between her and happiness even if she leaves a voice-recorder attached to a telephone in the room she has most recently vacated. It's like putting backbones in the fridge.

Tell me about it, people say to indicate that they know the story already.

Yesterday was like an ordinary run-of-the-mill comic book in black and white. I mean, one frame was alienated from the next. I never felt my denials more intensely. I went to church in a dirty train depot to wash away the sweat and think. In the public worship hole the meditation booths are often slimy, refuse litters the rim of the toilet bowl, and a stink floats between door and wall, making it impossible to get past the noxious to the pure. This is where the word "pew" was probably born.

I talk too much and prayed that God would help me practice silence. In the booth I remembered that Joseph speaks rarely in heaven, Mary even more rarely, and Jesus not at all. I remembered a realization that I once remembered after realizing the same thing several times and always forgetting that I had. It had to do with heaven being the Xian version of enlightenment. That's all I can recall.

Out in the fresh air I hurried down the streets, hearing my soul whisper: "No name. No passport. No money. No identification. No map. No home."

If you are the handmaiden of Zero, you will soon discover that Its manifestations of uncreated energy must be acknowledged whenever possible. Prayer is effective when it is directed towards the universe as a massive machine, and not towards an airy idea of Maker. After all, when Maker turns into Taker, you hate hate hate It. Better to recognize the materials as fixed, even when invisible to the naked eye. There is no escaping the universe.

Starlet

That terrible day my heart took a blow that nearly killed
it. While silver lilac shivered in the Hollywood Hills,
I packed and prepared to fly. My heart, once red as a
valentine, seemed to contract and blacken like a prune.

If you want to know the truth, I missed happiness by
inches. A meeting (planned for seven years) never took
place. The person lost me. I could not find him. As a
result, my personal pulse dropped the formula for
survival. I fled the city of colors, emptying, with each
mile, my will to go on.

On the night freeway my heart felt like a body in a pine
box, calling "Preacher, keep it short, for God's sake."

Every minute was a sort of monument in a mortuary.

1. To be lost is to be undiscovered.
2. To find is to discover what was already lost and waiting.

But where is the object of desire in fact?
Is it really out there, waiting?
How can it be there, when it requires time to find it?
And if the time required to get there doesn't yet exist, how
do I know it's there at all?

One Crossed Out

The walk up La Breaking to the Hills,
then a shortcut to rosemary and wild foresight. Walked her
    burning around.
Pining along the sandbags. Silhouettes of animals gave her joy.
Whose trunks and snouts are those on that reproducing zero?
In a basin seamy dried-up dams gave little hot tips of fuschia to
    redfingered men.
Peacock's things and a fish with a yellow nose were really not those,
    but like them.
"I want to return to start one, a new world I mean."
A thin path to the sea. Views on a promenade with lemonade looking
    for a place
to hang up her towel, shade for her lunch box, a plastic pint of mace
and water of course to swim in.
Now the night rain turns into rice
and in the morning paper covers the ground.
She hates that she meant it when she wrote: "Yes, unfortunately,
    still you."

He called the operating table a silver screen.
His face was reflected in the knife
where he could see she was a cut above seaweed but not
    tough enough
for such savagery. She climbed away like Jackie Kennedy.
But he kept calling her back. "Shorty! Say something!"
South Africans and North Americans of varying extractions
    were hunched at a table,
eating and doing fractions with golden Krugerrands.
They were as high as their IQs could go.
While the nurses there learned to hate experience, the doctors
    were so good
they didn't rape the women or kill the children until it was time
    for war.
Then they became vicious Humpty Dumptys in fatigues.
And the women couldn't get up again.
Red not being the least impression
of the whole occasion.
Slavery could still be seen swimming at the bottom of the petri dish.

In her palms were bread crumbs from a baguette, like little
    brown leaves.
A statue of Chaplin held the globe on his finger
atop someone's monument.
Nearby dried flowers hung over tins and brown bags dripped like
    potato skins.
Lunch hour for the grave diggers
for whom praxis and theory bring dreary consequences,
slamming around the granite,
gray yawnings over error, action, error, action. . . .
Now she dropped her sandwich
and fell to her knees. On the side of that stone was written NO WIN.
To NOT see this slogan was to win.
Second to be, second to be born, second to have
the first one's words in her ears, first to see the first one's warnings.
Like a ribbon snapping far from her hand.
"And" is the first word in Deuteronomy.

He was having a bank interview
for those terrified minutes when she could see
the horizon of reason.
Yellow-dipped maple leaf on a pavement smutted with dust, a haze,
congested traffic, and an aisle for dogs.
Under emotional conditions she can't ever run to catch anything.
Later in the rear seat of a car the man who wore dark glasses at night
remarked that her breathing was hard.
A walkbridge across the river led to a health bookstore
where she hoped they were going.
She hated hope when she knew she couldn't kill it
but it was as if Peter Pan's shadow was hanging from her drawers.
Or big flat American cotton underwear.
Watch it, Sugar, he said to her.
What is produced is greater than the value of the time spent
    producing it.

The present wears an implacable face. It won't budge,
just like the wall of water at the bottom of La Broken, a beach town.
Why does the water line up like a wall, it stays solid blue, and the
    present too.
Try to cut your way through it to another vista and you still have
    to splash
through the waves of today's givens into the next system.
You can't leap over the present because of its beauty!
A perfect structure, no matter where you look, all the shapes
    seem right.
That's why when you lose someone in it, someone you like,
the insurmountability of the present can cause you to go insane
with hate. I mean, you can build a target and aim for destruction.
You stop seeing what is in front of you, you hear neither yes nor no,
    but keep hoping
you will be in "the right place at the right time"
to find what's missing from everything complete.

Next time I'm motoring. Poplars are pinned to the last greens
but white olive leaves fly free.
Disappointments have gutted my gold lights.
Like paper poppies on counters in hotel lobbies,
the meaning of one is nothing, when they commemorate a day like
    Flanders Field.
That was the day the law went off and bayonets fell from numb
    shoulders, soldiers' eyes
turned to alabaster, guards turned into statues, and a man whirled on
    his axis.
Sometimes they test people with questions to which all the answers
    are wrong.
And then they like to create a market of temptations when there is no
    more need
for anything. They say things like, "This one's for victims of
    crucifixion.
The same is for wounds from contamination."
They tell you it's better to give something away than to lose it,
and then they take it. Those were the people who pursued their
    own ends
and owned all the means at the same time.
Next time I'm canceling.

I repressed my second self till it felt like a violent cadaver in my chest.
Then I took daily communism as a way to help and wrote for
      children
who couldn't read yet. I made them follow the sequence
until all the material
was bundled into an airless book.
Smears of cream looked like hankies on our brows by the end.
It was the old days, sickened women.
We had no price so we belonged to no market.
When I slipped past pub crawlers and puddles they evaporated
      at the same rate
as my feet.
No one asked: "Who's there?"
Not not.
"Not what? Not who?"
Not not you, but not not me either. Here or then.

Nobody wants crossed-out girls around.
Any agreement with them is difficult to achieve.
Hanging in hammocks all day, they only know how to wisecrack.
And with whatever happens to be the meaning of their days—
    they will make a pact.
A sneaker hangs in their trees.
They say things like "I'm not who's who in America. Are you?"
No, I'm just here with my corpse.
Double overalls like fences endlessly trespassing and nobody
saying thanks for everything.
Were these the pants I kicked in the air? one of them might ask.
To the fish, a person is a fish. But a crossed-out girl is always
    just that.
One has a teddy bear that looks like Ireland on a map.
Others beg a way out of their jobs from the boss.
Then one of them suddenly gets up one day and acts.
She will work as a labor union organizer beginning with female
    laundry workers.
Another will make jam when the raspberries strike.
And with her bellows a third will make the flames rise to beat down
    the damp
and raise up the poor. A bunch will raise five children who aren't
    white.
I am wishing for this way to happen fast.
Dreams have orientation. Dreams like women who are bad.

The Mohawk Special shovels up
the lace of an elephant's ear. (That's what the frozen ground is like.)
This is the year when half of my desire for you is the half of yours for
    someone else.
It's the time when the working class means the unemployed.
The girl with the mandolin plays her catgut strings—for all of us—
until the trees outside are singing "Eurydice is back!"
(She was waiting for the Godblack Shine to arrive.)
A person is never in more distress than near the finish.
It's the same year when a spot of gin means warmth
for pinning papers on the cold street poles.
Not so long ago a body carried its own profile chart and rules.
A species of radio waves has replaced actual passengers
with a stillness even without birds.
Still the mystery of your life is that it's yours.
What are the indications? Rest and speech. Silhouettes of beasts.
The pearls will roll, you'll see.

The Low Road

Soon she headed into the wind. Sepulveda Boulevard would lead her to the cornfields and crows of Scripture, a field gullied by rainfall, and parking lots where men sat in cars smoking. Sometimes they got out of their cars and went to the bathroom in a cement barrack. This action scared her back to creation. Rows of electric lights burned white in the daylight under a plastic tent. A model airplane buzzed across the field, but she was forbidden entrance to that nature preserve because she walked with a dog. Encircled by mountains, the valley was a catcher for fog. Early mist dreamed over the dam. Brittle twigs screened her vista. Berries bled blue but were gray with dew too. Two bodies had lain in mud the night before as she bolted across the San Diego Freeway. Yellow canvas covered them and she flinched to avoid a blue raindrop heading for her eye. Police lights were on the way. She had noticed earlier that angels, like mourning doves, coo to a Pyhrric meter. Later she would take the square bread soaked in wine from an Eastern Orthodox priest and pray for those bodies. But that night she continued on past the end of their lives to the recycling center with her daily bag of cans.

Everything's a Fake

Coyote scruff in canyons off Mulholland Drive. Fragrance of sage and rosemary, now it's spring. At night the mockingbirds ring their warnings of cats coming across the neighborhoods. Like castanets in the palms of a dancer, the palm trees clack. The HOLLYWOOD sign has a white skin of fog across it where erotic canyons hump, moisten, slide, dry up, swell, and shift. They appear impatient—to make such powerful contact with pleasure that they will toss back the entire cover of earth. She walks for days around brown trails, threading sometimes under the low branches of bay and acacia. Bitter flowers will catch her eye: pink and thin honeysuckle, or mock orange. They coat the branches like lace in the back of a mystical store. Other deviant men and women live at the base of these canyons, closer to the city however. Her mouth is often dry, her chest tight, but she is filled to the brim with excess idolatry. It was like a flat mouse—the whole of Los Angeles she could hold in the circle formed by her thumb and forefinger. Tires were planted to stop the flow of mud at her feet. But she could see all the way to Long Beach through a tunnel made in her fist. Her quest for the perfect place was only a symptom of the same infection that was out there, a mild one, but a symptom nonetheless.

There Are No "Others"

Outside the plant they walked hurriedly, she a few paces behind him, her voice raw and loud. Her right hand held tight to the swinging bed for baby, invisible in a mashed potato-ish heap of cottons and quilts. The man was dressed entirely in black, wore a tight black net on his hair, sweated lightly through his dewy black skin. Her bleached yellow hair expressed no cowardice, but rage, so they both (because together) suffered all the way from the plant to the car. "What kind of girl is this—an empty shell? a lonely cell in which an empty soul must dwell?" Colors are idenitified with the state of the spirit. The Regency Arms for example were red in welcoming her every night, both as anarchist arms and as sexual arms. Red lips on a tropical neon sign read REAL LIVE NUDES. Mini-malls held gourmet shops along Sunset Boulevard. Her talk all the way to the click of the car door was really a scream. Why was he taking it so passively? others wondered watching. But in such a case there are no others. Dog piss on a rhododendron bush meantime wet a small piece of script reading JESUS COSMOS. It was the Sabbath when all things begin anew, and all things are considered equal, and when, as in dreams, the new and the equal know no evil.

The Bourgeoisie Despises Poverty
and Denies It Cultural Validity

A trough inside the Pacific Ocean led to an onshore flow. Then high seas, large swells, and a small-craft advisory. One storm system was weaker than the one before, and so did nothing to shift around the ozone, carbon monoxide, nitrogen dioxide, or the premenstrual syndrome in women's bodies. From the Southland mountains into the valley, clouds pumped out shadows and rainbows. Palm leaves played on invisible keys, and the only children on the streets of Hollywood were lost children. Just as jazz makes white wine chill on a balcony, so black stockings make syringes look like silver, and nostril rings resemble Disney tattoos. Shelter couches have rough skins and are not welcoming. Leather gloves, rip-hemmed jeans, sneakers, and Benadryl, all for sale. Kiss my casket, said one of nine thousand inmates. Two thousand have been given antibiotics against an outbreak of meningitis. One individual lay on a mattress in an unlighted cell, listening. It had to be a detour he was experiencing. He had hoped for notoriety when the means of his survival was found in obscurity. When he had begun performing actions that he knew were expected of him, he had already begun to lose his way. Now protected by darkness that his interior met with lighted, colorized dream stories, he could live without gas or refrigeration. He had come to this condition without even making a choice. It was rather as if someone had stuck up a sign in a lonely highway, and he had obeyed it, although it turned out to have been a joke intended for someone else to laugh about.

You Can't Warm Your Hands in Front of a Book but You Can Warm Your Hopes There

Feathers fluffed the ashtray bin at the bottom of the elevator. Feathers and a smeared black look littered the parking lot like mascara. A cage would glide back and let them out to merge with the other cars on La Brea. It looked as if a struggle had ended in tears between the bird and an enemy. She broke through the fear to examine it. No chicken claws, or comb, no wing, no egg. The neutrality of words like "nothing" and "silence" vibrated at her back like plastic drapes. How could there be a word for silence? A child's lips might blow, the North wind bring snow, a few stars explode, boats rock, but whatever moved in air did not by necessity move in ears and require the word "silence" therefore. She had personally sunk to a level where she could produce thought, and only "violence" remained a problem. It was common in her circle. A bush could turn into a fire, or a face at a clap of the hand could release spit and infection. The deviants were like herself unable to control their feelings. Los Angeles for them was only hostile as a real situation during the rainy season when torrents ripped down the sides of the canyons and overnight turned them sloshy. Then they hid in underground places, carrying *Must the Morgue be my Only Shelter??* signs. But the rest of the time the sort of whiteness spread out by a Southland sun kept them warm, and they could shit whenever they wanted to, in those places they had long ago staked out. My personal angel is my maid, said one to another, putting down his Rilke with a gentle smile.

My Song, My Only Song Goes:

One is my lucky number! Her sneakers were wearing down to two gnarled scoops, but she was never surprised that the vertical pronoun was also a number. On the apophatic path you choose to stay at the edge of the central city where you get a quasi-this and a quasi-that. In the diplomatic world transparency means nonideological, neutral. In the walking world, it means eternal, invisible. One day clouds muffin against a tinny sky. L.A.'s a dirt heap, really, stuck with green nettles. A better shape to live in than the slabbish city. Cold and square as Forest Lawn. Why put a cake on a plate before putting it in your mouth? Why use a napkin instead of a sleeve to wipe away the dribble? I mean when I was walking the streets, she couldn't conceive of her own loneliness. Captain-bass-playing melodies got to it, though, a black sax, like a footbridge over cognac. New York is a whole deal. Yoni, sacred as a red anarchist, was given to every woman. Even the stepsister could say it twice. And her stepsister would say, exactly the way she would, "My stepsister hoped I would die." B-minus was her score. She began by a drink or three to keep her moving down lubricated avenues. There the faces of brown-skinned boys presented her with the problem of beauty. Africa refused to leave them alone in America. For this great act of mercy she was happy: for them there would be no erasure! Their beauty was a promise that couldn't be broken, it was Adam getting Even, it was as basic as a billy club. Let the academics sneer at the Jesuits, and go on being the hypocritical clerics of the century, she at least dared to believe in retribution. While one derelict liked malt, barley, and high altitudes, most of the others like herself preferred a cloud of mimosa breaking down the chickenwire and feet firmly planted on the names of the stars embossed in Hollywood Boulevard. She had her private "names for the days of the weak"—Man Day, Dues Day, Wine Day, Thirst Day, Fried Day, Sat-Around Day, and the Sabbath. These were written in the earthball under her body's weight, where she was pleased to keep them.

The Apophatic Path

1.
What isn't what is

not Discover me!
or Try to find me.

If being is finding,

can you find me?
Who to, this address?

. . .

Being as close to a shadow
as a color

what isn't
is what is

and I can't see
but know as no.

Non amari sed amare.

. . .

Or will a question be,

"Is the discovery for real me?"

Signature a stone???

Like what isn't
is what is

when not being
ever ever ever found!

2.

Basic science

will blend ghostness
among enemies.

Now bodies cemented

down in monster denominations
to be counted

one of the walking
corpses I see whitening

and emptying
under a sun

makes me know me
to be no one.

3.

Walk to developmental old trombone—I—

seeking to be found—
inside time!—by one whose blues

seek by speaking tunes to
this specific city afternoon

of bread, fumes, and orange
nasturtiums—am, still, solo—

even the base of me being, unknown.

The text of *One Crossed Out* is set in a typeface known as Old Style Number Seven, which dates to a time when typefaces bore generic names rather than descriptive or fanciful ones. The roots of Old Style Number Seven can be found in the middle of the nineteenth century at the Miller & Richard type foundry in Edinburgh. At that time, Scottish founders led the way in cutting sturdy, even-colored types to meet the demands of new generations of printing presses. Down to the present day, Old Style Number Seven has continued to survive technology shifts.

The book was designed by Will Powers, set in type by Stanton Publication Services, Inc., and manufactured by Malloy Lithographing, Inc. on acid-free paper.